Make Your Mind an Ocean

MAY THE BUDDHADHARMA REACH ALL SENTIENT BEINGS · LAMA YESHE WISDOM ARCHIVE ·

Previously published by the LAMA YESHE WISDOM ARCHIVE

Becoming Your Own Therapist, by Lama Yeshe
Advice for Monks and Nuns, by Lama Yeshe and Lama Zopa Rinpoche
Virtue and Reality, by Lama Zopa Rinpoche
Teachings from the Vajrasattva Retreat, by Lama Zopa Rinpoche

For initiates only:
A Chat about Heruka, by Lama Zopa Rinpoche
A Chat about Yamantaka, by Lama Zopa Rinpoche

Forthcoming in 2000
Making Life Meaningful, by Lama Zopa Rinpoche
*The Essence of Tibetan Buddhism: The Three Principal Aspects of the Path
and An Introduction to Tantra,* by Lama Yeshe

(Contact us for information)

*May whoever sees, touches, reads, remembers, or talks or thinks about these
booklets never be reborn in unfortunate circumstances, receive only rebirths
in situations conducive to the perfect practice of Dharma, meet only perfectly
qualified spiritual guides, quickly develop bodhicitta and immediately
attain enlightenment for the sake of all sentient beings.*

Lama Yeshe

Make Your Mind an Ocean

Aspects of Buddhist Psychology

Edited by Nicholas Ribush

Lama Yeshe Wisdom Archive • Boston

www.LamaYeshe.com

A non-profit charitable organization for the benefit of all
sentient beings and a section of the Foundation for the
Preservation of the Mahayana Tradition
www.fpmt.org

First published 1999
10,000 copies for free distribution
Second printing 2000, 12,000

LAMA YESHE WISDOM ARCHIVE
PO BOX 356
WESTON
MA 02493 USA

ISBN 1-891868-03-9

10 9 8 7 6 5 4 3 2

Cover photographs by Jacqueline Keeley

Printed in Canada on recycled, acid-free paper

Please contact the LAMA YESHE WISDOM ARCHIVE for copies of
our free booklets

CONTENTS

EDITOR'S INTRODUCTION   11

YOUR MIND IS YOUR RELIGION   13

A BUDDHIST APPROACH TO MENTAL ILLNESS   29

EVERYTHING COMES FROM THE MIND   45

MAKE YOUR MIND AN OCEAN   51

PUBLISHER'S ACKNOWLEDGMENTS

We are extremely grateful to our friends and supporters who have made it possible for the LAMA YESHE WISDOM ARCHIVE to both exist and function. To Lama Yeshe and Lama Zopa Rinpoche, whose kindness is impossible to repay. To Peter and Nicole Kedge and Venerable Ailsa Cameron for helping bring the ARCHIVE to its present state of development. To Venerable Roger Kunsang, Lama Zopa's tireless assistant, for his kindness and consideration. And to our sustaining supporters: Drs. Penny Noyce & Leo Liu, Barry & Connie Hershey, Joan Terry, Roger & Claire Ash-Wheeler, Henry & Catherine Lau, Claire Atkins, Ecie Hursthouse, Lily Chang Wu, Nancy Pan, Thubten Yeshe Alexander, Therese Miller, Tom & Suzanne Castles, Datuk Tai Tsu Kuang, Chuah Kok Leng, the Caytons (Lori, Karuna, Pam, Bob & Amy), Claire Ritter, Tom Thorning, Wisdom Books (London), Tan Swee Eng, Salim Lee, Richard Gere, Cecily Drucker, Lynnea Elkind, Janet Moore, Su Hung, Carol Davies and Lorenzo Vassallo.

We are also grateful to those generous contributors who responded to the request for funds we made in our last mailing, October, 1999. Therefore, for donations received up to the end of February, 2000, we extend a huge thank you to Diana Abrashkin, Harmony Adkins, Kate & Chris Aitken, Dean Alper, Ben & Deb Alterman, Margie Amick, Amitabha Buddhist Centre, Anne Amos, Roger Amos, Leticia Anson,

Ruben Anton, Steve Armstrong, Isabel Arocena, Atisha Centre, Charlotte Avant, Faith Bach, Luke Bailey, Peter Baker, Judi Beardsley, Kerstin Beck, David Bellos, Jacalyn Bennett, Peggy Bennington, Bradley Black, Allan Bomhard, Andrew Bordwin, Siliana Bosa (for the good rebirth of Vincenzo Grazioli), Betsy Bourdon, Robyn Brentano & Bill Kelley, Robert & Anne Britton, René & Marguerite Brochard, Ross Brooke, Don Brown, Pamela Butler, Carolyn Byrne, Claudia Callan, Jennifer Campanelli, Mark Campbell, Felix Carabello, Margaret Carmier, Laura Carter, Steve & Polly Casmar, Zachary Casper, Jack and Trena Cerveri, Chandrakirti Meditation Centre, Vicki Chen, June Cheng, Thubten Chönyid, Ngawang Chötak, Robin Coleman, Gavriella Conn, Bryan Cooper, Doug Crane & Deje Zhoga, Eleanor Cusick, Maryann Czermak, Daniel De Biasi, Nan Deal, Ricardo de Aratanha, Linda de Witt & Robert Green, Bhikkhu Dhammassava, Laure Dillon, Cecily Drucker, John Dunne & Sara McClintock, Ken & Malou Dusyn, Joseph Dynh, Dzogchen Foundation, Keith Emmons, Adam Engle, Donna Estess, Richard Farris, Adriana Ferranti, Ven. René Feusi, Martha Foster, Sesame Fowler, Terry Fralich & Rebecca Wing, Claudia Frey, Robert & Sheryl Friedman, Marianne Fritz, Lynn Gebetsberger, Eileen Gebrian, Nancy Gibson, Kathleen Glomski, Julio Gonzalez, Judy & Ian Green, Sandy Grindlay, Worth Gurkin, Lucile Hamlin, Bernard Handler, Wyatt Harlan, Margi Haas, Richard Hay, Jane Hein, Graziella Heins, Myron Helmer, Christine Hether, W. Bosco Ho, Lisa Hochman, Larry Howe & Martha Tack, Ken Huber, Victoria Huckenpahler, Walter Illes, Elaine Jackson, James Johns, Ven. Tenzin Kachö, Toni Kenyon, Eric Klaft, Nicholas Kolivas, Camille Kozlowski, Lorne & Terry Ladner, Mim Lagoe, Tony Lagreca, Chiu Mei Lai, Ven. Chiu Min Lai, Chiu

Nan Lai, Laurence Laubsher, Alfred Leyens, Ven. Trime Lhamo, John Liberty, Li Lightfoot, Judy Lin, Ludovico Lopez Cadé, Sue Lucksted-Tharp, Kendall Magnussen, Beth Magura, John & Barbara Makransky, Lenard Martin, Doss McDavid, Amy McKhann, Diego Melendez, Menkit, Elea & Michael Mideke, Amy Miller, Lynda Millspaugh, Zbigniew Modrzejewski, Marilyn Montgomery, Theobold Mordey, Paula Moreau, Jack Morison, Kalleen Mortensen, Dolores Moses, Ada Mundo, Steve Nahaczewski, Stacy O'Leary, Ann Parker, Michele Paterson, David Patt, Nancy Patton, Dennis Paulson, Justin Pollard, Jacek Pollner, Ellen Powell, George Propps, Janyce Reidel, Leslie Reincke, Isabel Resano, Mariette Risley, John Ross, Carol Royce-Wilder, Elaine Rysner, Jesse Sartain, Priscilla Sawa, Robert Schense, Victoria Scott, Brian Selius, Jhampa Shaneman, Rosa Shen, Kim Shetter, Susan Shore, Beth Simon, Yolanda Snell, Lynne Sonenberg, Nova Spivak, Elin Steinthorsdottir, Kay Stewart, Hans & Helga Steyskal, Sarah Stiles, Dawn Stracener, Susan Stumpf, Laurie Sulzer, Lana Sundberg, Sandra Tatlock, Debra Thornburg, Thubten Kunga Center, Jessica Torres, Ven. Charles Trebaol, Vajrasattva Mountain Centre, Wendy vanden Heuvel, Diana van Die, Barbara Vautier, Chris Vautier, Lynn Wade, Tom Waggoner, Shasta Wallace, Sylvia Wasek, Lila & Joel Weinberg, Matthew Weiss, Judith Weitzner, Silvia Wenger, Jane Werner, Kate Lila Wheeler, Bonda White, Cat Wilson, Loren Wilson, Louie Bob Wood, Soo Hwa Yeo and Ven. Sarah Tenzin Yiwong.

Finally, we would also like to thank the many kind people who have asked that their donations be kept anonymous and the volunteers who have given so generously of their time to help us with our mailings.

If you, dear reader, would like to join this noble group of open-hearted altruists by contributing to the production of more free booklets by Lama Yeshe or Lama Zopa Rinpoche or to any other aspect of the LAMA YESHE WISDOM ARCHIVE'S work, please contact us to find out how.

Through the merit of having contributed to the spread of the Buddha's teachings for the sake of all sentient beings, may our benefactors and their families and friends have long and healthy lives, all happiness, and may all their Dharma wishes be instantly fulfilled.

Editor's Introduction

In the LAMA YESHE WISDOM ARCHIVE's first booklet, Lama Yeshe's *Becoming Your Own Therapist*, I mentioned the unique qualities of Lama Yeshe's teachings. *Make Your Mind an Ocean* again makes evident just how special Lama's teachings were.

The talks in this booklet are on the general topic of the mind and were given during Lama Yeshe's and Lama Zopa Rinpoche's second world tour, in 1975. I had the great honor of accompanying the Lamas on this tour and was present at all these discourses. Most of the people who attended were new to Buddhism and had never seen a Tibetan lama before, a situation quite different from what we find today. As ever, Lama's timeless wisdom shines through, and his teachings are as relevant today as they were back then.

Two of these talks were lunchtime lectures at Melbourne and Latrobe Universities. The latter started a bit late, so there was no time to finish with the usual question and answer session that Lama liked so much. The chapter "Make Your Mind an Ocean" was an evening lecture given to the general public and attended by several hundred people.

Of greatest interest, perhaps, is "A Buddhist Approach to Mental Illness." Here Lama met with a group of psychiatrists at Prince Henry's Hospital, which was at that time a teaching hospital connected with Monash University Medical School. Prior to that it had been affiliated with Melbourne University, and Prince Henry's was where I studied my clinical medicine and worked for several years after graduation. Thus, several of the psychiatrists with whom Lama met that afternoon were former teachers and colleagues of mine, and apart from anything else, I was interested to observe their reaction to my outer transformation (I was in monk's robes at the time). The hospital was demolished a few years ago; the last time I drove by it was but a hole in the ground, a symbol of how much has changed since those halcyon days. Anyway, these doctors were delighted to meet and question Lama, and this historic exchange underscores the difference between Western and Buddhist concepts of mental health.

I would like to thank Rand Engel, Victoria Fremont, Christina Russo and Wendy Cook for their excellent editorial input, and Mark and Linda Gatter for their help with the design and production of this booklet.

Your Mind is Your Religion

When I talk about mind, I'm not just talking about my mind, my trip. I'm talking about the mind of each and every universal living being.

The way we live, the way we think—everything is dedicated to material pleasure. We consider sense objects to be of utmost importance and materialistically devote ourselves to whatever makes us happy, famous or popular. Even though all this comes from our mind, we are so totally preoccupied by external objects that we never look within, we never question why we find them so interesting.

As long as we exist, our mind is an inseparable part of us. As a result, we are always up and down. It is not our body that goes up and down, it's our mind—this mind whose way of functioning we do not understand. Therefore, sometimes we have to examine ourselves—not just our body, but our mind. After all, it is our mind that is always telling us what to do. We have to know our own psychology, or, in religious terminology, perhaps, our inner nature. Anyway, no matter what we call it, we have to know our own mind.

Don't think that examining and knowing the nature of your mind is just an Eastern trip. That's a wrong conception. It's your trip. How can you separate your body, or your self-image, from your mind? It's impossible. You think you are an independent person, free to travel the world, enjoying everything. Despite what you think, you are not free. I'm not saying that you are under the control of someone else. It's your own uncontrolled mind, your own attachment, that oppresses you. If you discover how you oppress yourself, your uncontrolled mind will disappear. Knowing your own mind is the solution to all your problems.

One day the world looks so beautiful; the next day it looks terrible. How can you say that? Scientifically, it's impossible that the world can change so radically. It's your mind that causes these appearances. This is not religious dogma; your up and down is not religious dogma. I'm not talking about religion; I'm talking about the way you lead your daily life, which is what sends you up and down. Other people and your environment don't change radically; it's your mind. I hope you understand that.

Similarly, one person thinks that the world is beautiful and people are wonderful and kind, while another thinks that everything and everyone are horrible. Who is right? How do you explain that scientifically? It's just their individual mind's projection of the sense world. You think, "Today is like this, tomorrow is like that; this man is like this; that woman is like that." But where is that absolutely fixed, forever-beautiful woman? Who is that absolutely forever-handsome man? They are non-existent—they are simply creations of your own mind.

Do not expect material objects to satisfy you or to make your life perfect; it's impossible. How can you be satisfied by even vast amounts of material objects? How will sleeping with hundreds of different people satisfy you? It will never happen. Satisfaction comes from the mind.

If you don't know your own psychology, you might ignore what's going on in your mind until it breaks down and you go completely crazy. People go mad through lack of inner wisdom, through their inability to examine their own minds. They cannot explain themselves to themselves; they don't know how to talk to themselves. Thus they are constantly preoccupied with all these external objects, while within, their minds are running down until they finally crack. They are ignorant of their internal world, and their minds are totally unified with ignorance instead of being awake and engaged in self-analysis. Examine your own mental attitudes. Become your own therapist.

You are intelligent; you know that material objects alone cannot bring you satisfaction, but you don't have to embark on some emotional, religious trip to examine your own mind. Some people think that they do; that this kind of self-analysis is something spiritual or religious. It's not necessary to classify yourself as a follower of this or that religion or philosophy, to put yourself into some religious category. But if you want to be happy, you have to check the way you lead your life. Your mind is your religion.

When you check your mind, do not rationalize or push. Relax. Do not be upset when problems arise. Just be aware of them and where they come from; know their root. Introduce the problem to yourself: "Here is this kind of problem. How has it become a problem? What kind of mind has made it a problem? What kind of mind feels that it's a problem?" When you check thoroughly, the problem will automatically disappear. That's so simple, isn't it? You don't have to believe in something. Don't believe anything! All the same, you can't say, "I don't believe I have a mind." You can't reject your mind. You can say, "I reject Eastern things"—I agree. But can you reject

15

yourself? Can you deny your head, your nose? You cannot deny your mind. Therefore, treat yourself wisely and try to discover the true source of satisfaction.

When you were a child you loved and craved ice-cream, chocolate and cake, and thought, "When I grow up, I'll have all the ice-cream, chocolate and cake I want; then I'll be happy." Now you have as much ice-cream, chocolate and cake as you want, but you're bored. You decide that since this doesn't make you happy you'll get a car, a house, television, a husband or wife—then you'll be happy. Now you have everything, but your car is a problem, your house is a problem, your husband or wife is a problem, your children are a problem. You realize, "Oh, this is not satisfaction."

What, then, is satisfaction? Go through all this mentally and check; it's very important. Examine your life from childhood to the present. This is analytical meditation: "At that time my mind was like that; now my mind is like this. It has changed this way, that way." Your mind has changed so many times but have you reached any conclusion as to what really makes you happy? My interpretation is that you are lost. You know your way around the city, how to get home, where to buy chocolate, but still you are lost—you can't find your goal. Check honestly—isn't this so?

Lord Buddha says that all you have to know is what you are, how you exist. You don't have to believe in anything. Just understand your mind: how it works, how attachment and desire arise, how ignorance arises, and where emotions come from. It is sufficient to know the nature of all that; that alone can bring you happiness and peace. Thus, your life can change completely; everything can turn upside down. What you once interpreted as horrible can become beautiful.

If I told you that all you were living for was chocolate and ice-cream, you'd think I was crazy. "No! no!" your arrogant mind would say. But look deeper into your life's purpose. Why are you here? To be well liked? To become famous? To accumulate possessions? To be attractive to others? I'm not exaggerating—check for yourself, then you'll see. Through thorough examination you can realize that dedicating your entire life to seeking happiness through chocolate and ice-cream completely nullifies the significance of your having been born human. Birds and dogs have similar aims. Shouldn't your goals in life be higher than those of dogs and chickens?

I'm not trying to decide your life for you, but you check up. It's better to have an integrated life than to live in mental disorder. A disorderly life is not worthwhile, beneficial to neither yourself nor others. What *are* you living for—chocolate? Steak? Perhaps you think, "Of course I don't live for food. I'm an educated person." But education also comes from the mind. Without the mind, what is education, what is philosophy? Philosophy is just the creation of someone's mind, a few thoughts strung together in a certain way. Without the mind there's no philosophy, no doctrine, no university subjects. All these things are mind-made.

How do you check your mind? Just watch how it perceives or interprets any object that it encounters. Observe what feelings—comfortable or uncomfortable—arise. Then check, "When I perceive this kind of view, this feeling arises, that emotion comes; I discriminate in such a way. Why?" This is how to check your mind; that's all. It's very simple.

When you check your own mind properly, you stop blaming others for your problems. You recognize that your mistaken actions come from your own defiled, deluded mind. When you are preoccupied with external, material objects, you blame them and other people for your problems. Projecting that deluded view onto external phenomena makes you miserable. When you begin to realize your wrong-conception view, you begin to realize the nature of your own mind and to put an end to your problems forever.

Is all this very new for you? It's not. Whenever you are going to do anything, you first check it out and then make your decision. You already do this; I'm not suggesting anything new. The difference is that you don't do it enough. You have to do more checking. This doesn't mean sitting alone in some corner contemplating your navel—you can be checking your mind all the time, even while talking or working with other people. Do you think that examining the mind is only for those who are on an Eastern trip? Don't think that way.

Realize that the nature of your mind is different from that of the flesh and bone of your physical body. Your mind is like a mirror, reflecting everything without discrimination. If you have understanding-wisdom, you can control the kind of reflection that you allow into the mirror of your mind. If you totally ignore what is happening in your mind, it will reflect whatever garbage it encounters—things that make you psychologically sick. Your checking-wisdom should distinguish between reflections that are beneficial and those that bring psychological problems. Eventually, when you realize the true nature of subject and object, all your problems will vanish.

Some people think they are religious, but what is religious? If you do not examine your own nature, do not gain knowledge-wisdom, how are you religious? Just the idea that you are religious—"I am Buddhist, Jewish, whatever"—does not help at all. It does not help you; it does not help others. In order to really help others, you need to gain knowledge-wisdom.

The greatest problems of humanity are psychological, not material. From birth to death, people are continuously under the control of their mental sufferings. Some people never keep watch on their minds when things are going well, but when something goes wrong—an accident or some other terrible experience—they immediately say, "God, please help me." They call themselves religious but it's a joke. In happiness or sorrow, a serious practitioner maintains constant awareness of God and one's own nature. You're not being realistic or even remotely religious if, when you are having a good time, surrounded by chocolate and preoccupied by worldly sense pleasures, you forget yourself, and turn to God only when something awful happens.

No matter which of the many world religions we consider, their interpretation of God or Buddha and so forth is simply words and mind; these two alone. Therefore, words don't matter so much. What you have to realize is that everything—good and bad, every philosophy and doctrine—comes from mind. The mind is very powerful. Therefore, it requires firm guidance. A powerful jet plane needs a good pilot; the pilot of your mind should be the wisdom that understands its nature. In that way, you can direct your powerful mental energy to benefit your life instead of letting it run about uncontrollably like a mad elephant, destroying yourself and others.

I don't need to say much more. I think you understand what I'm talking about. At this point a little dialog would be more useful. Ask questions; I'll try to answer. Remember that you don't have to agree with what I say. You have to understand my attitude, my mind. If you don't like what I've been saying, please contradict me. I like people to argue with me. I'm not a dictator: "You people should do this; you people should do that." I can't tell you what to do. I make suggestions; what I want is for you to check up. If you do that, I'll be satisfied. So tell me if you disagree with what I've said.

Q: How do you check up on your own mind? How do you do it?

Lama: A simple way of checking up on your own mind is to investigate how you perceive things, how you interpret your experiences. Why do you have so many different feelings about your boyfriend even during the course of one day? In the morning you feel good about him, in the afternoon, kind of foggy; why is that? Has your boyfriend changed that radically from morning to afternoon? No, there's been no radical change, so why do you feel so differently about him? That's the way to check.

Q: If you can't trust your mind to make a decision, can you leave it to something outside? Like telling yourself, "If such and such happens, I'll go here; if something else happens, I'll go there."

Lama: Before you do anything, you should ask yourself why you are doing it, what is your purpose; what course of action you are embarking on. If the path ahead seems troublesome, perhaps you shouldn't take it; if it looks worthwhile, you can probably proceed. First, check up. Don't act without knowing what's in store for you.

Q: What's a lama?

Lama: Good question. From the Tibetan point of view, a lama is someone who is extremely well educated in the internal world and knows not only the present mind but also the past and the future.

Psychologically speaking, a lama can see where he has come from and where he's going. He also has the power to control himself and the ability to offer psychological advice to others. Tibetans would consider anyone like that to be a lama.

Q: What would be the equivalent of a lama in the West?

Lama: I don't know that we have the exact equivalent here. It could be some kind of combination of priest, psychologist and doctor. But as I just said, a lama has realized the true nature of his own and others' minds and can offer perfect solutions to others' mental problems. I'm not criticizing them, but I doubt that many Western psychologists have the same degree of understanding of the mind or the emotional problems that people experience. Sometimes they offer somewhat poor quality, superficial explanations for the problems people are going through, such as, "When you were a child your mother did this, your father did that..." I disagree; it's not true. You can't blame your parents for your problems like that. Of course, environmental factors can contribute to difficulties, but the principal cause is always within you; the basic problem is never outside. I don't know, but perhaps Western doctors are too afraid to interpret things in this way. Also, I have met many priests, some of whom are my friends, but they tend not to deal too much with the here and now. Instead of focusing on practical ways of coping with everyday uncertainties, they emphasize religious considerations such as God, faith and so forth. But people today tend to be skeptical and often reject the help that some priests can offer.

Q: How does meditation help you make decisions?

Lama: Meditation works because it is not a method that requires you to believe in something but rather one that you can put into action for yourself. You check, or watch, your own mind. If someone's giving you a hard time and your ego starts to hurt, instead of reacting, just take a look at what's going on. Think of how sound is simply coming out of the other person's mouth, entering your ear, and causing pain in your heart. If you think about this in the right way, it will make you laugh; you will see how ridiculous it is to get upset by something so insubstantial. Then your problem will disappear—poof! Just like that. By practicing in this way, you will discover through your own experience how meditation helps and how it offers satisfactory solutions to all your problems. Meditation is not words, it's wisdom.

Q: Lama, could you please talk a little about karma.

Lama: Sure: *you are karma.* It's that simple. Actually, karma is a Sanskrit word that, roughly translated, means cause and effect. What does that mean? Yesterday something happened in your mind; today you experience the effect. Or, your environment: you have certain parents, you live in a certain situation, all that has an effect on you. As you go through life, every day, everything you do, all the time, within your mind there's a constant chain of cause and reaction, cause and reaction; that's karma. As long as you're in your body, interacting with the sense world, discriminating this is good, that is bad, your mind is automatically creating karma, cause and effect. Karma is not just theoretical philosophy, it's science, Buddhist science. Karma explains how life evolves; form and feeling, color and sensation, discrimination; your entire life, what you are, where you come from, how you keep going, your relationship with your mind. Karma is

Buddhism's scientific explanation of evolution. So, even though karma is a Sanskrit word, actually, *you are* karma, your whole life is controlled by karma, you live within the energy field of karma. Your energy interacts with another energy, then another, and another, and that's how your entire life unfolds. Physically, mentally, it's all karma. Therefore, karma isn't something you have to believe in. Because of the characteristic nature of your mind and body, you are constantly circling through the six realms of cyclic existence, whether you believe in karma or not. In the physical universe, when everything comes together—earth, sea, the four elements, heat and so forth—effects automatically result; there's no need for belief to know this happens. It's the same thing in your internal universe, especially when you're in contact with the sense world; you're constantly reacting. For example, last year you enjoyed delicious chocolate with much attachment but haven't had any since, so you miss it badly, "Oh, I'd really love some chocolate." You remember your previous experience of chocolate; that memory causes you to crave and grasp for more. That reaction to your previous experience is karma; the experience is the cause, the missing is the result. It's actually quite simple.

Q: What is your purpose in life?
Lama: You're asking me about my purpose in life? That's something for me to check for myself, but if I had to reply, I'd say my purpose is to dedicate myself as much as I possibly can to the welfare of others, while trying to be of benefit to myself as well. I can't say that I'm succeeding in any of this, but those are my aims.

Q: Is the mind different from the soul? When you speak of solving the problems of the mind, do you mean that the mind is the problem and not the soul?

Lama: Philosophically, the soul can be interpreted in a number of ways. In Christianity and Hinduism, the soul is different from the mind and is considered to be something permanent and self-existent. In my opinion, there's no such thing. In Buddhist terminology, the soul, mind or whatever you call it is ever-changing, impermanent. I don't really make a distinction between mind and soul, but within yourself you can't find anything that's permanent or self-existent. With respect to mental problems, don't think that the mind is totally negative; it's the uncontrolled mind that causes problems. If you develop the right kind of wisdom and thereby recognize the nature of the uncontrolled mind, it will automatically disappear. But until you do, the uncontrolled mind will completely dominate you.

Q: I've heard many times that many Westerners can grasp the philosophy of Tibetan Buddhism intellectually but have difficulty in putting it into practice. It makes sense to them but they can't integrate it with their lives. What do you think the block is?

Lama: That's a great question, thank you. Tibetan Buddhism teaches you to overcome your dissatisfied mind, but to do that you have to make an effort. To put our techniques into your own experience, you have to go slowly, gradually. You can't just jump right in the deep end. It takes time and we expect you to have trouble at first. But if you take it easy it gets less and less difficult as time goes by.

Q: What is our mind's true nature and how do we go about recognizing it?

Lama: There are two aspects to the mind's nature, the relative and the absolute. The relative is the mind that perceives and functions in the sense world. We also call that mind dualistic and because of what I describe as its "that-this" perception, it is totally agitated in nature. However, by transcending the dualistic mind, you can unify your view. At that time you realize the absolute true nature of the mind, which is totally beyond the duality. In dealing with the sense world in our normal, everyday, mundane life, two things always appear. The appearance of two things always creates a problem. It's like children— one alone is OK, two together always make trouble. Similarly, as our five senses interpret the world and supply dualistic information to our mind, our mind grasps at that view, and that automatically causes conflict and agitation. This is the complete opposite of the experience of inner peace and freedom. Therefore, by reaching beyond that you will experience perfect peace. Now, this is just a short reply to what you asked and perhaps it's unsatisfactory, because it's a big question. What I've said is merely a simple introduction to a profound topic. However, if you have some background in this subject, my answer might satisfy you.

Q: When you check your mind, does it always tell you the truth?
Lama: No, not necessarily. Sometimes your wrong conceptions answer. You shouldn't listen to them. Instead, you have to tell yourself, I'm not satisfied with what that mind says; I want a better answer. You have to keep checking more and more deeply until your wisdom responds. But it's good to question; if you don't ask questions, you'll never get any answers. But you shouldn't ask emotionally, Oh, what's that, what's that, what's that? I have to find out; I have to know. If

you have a question, write it down; think about it carefully. Gradually the right answer will come. It takes time. If you don't get an answer today, stick the question on your fridge. If you question strongly, answers will come, sometimes even in dreams. Why will you get answers? Because your basic nature is wisdom. Don't think that you're hopelessly ignorant. Human nature has both positive and negative aspects.

Q: What is your definition of a guru?

Lama: A guru is a person who can really show you the true nature of your mind and who knows the perfect remedies for your psychological problems. Someone who doesn't know his own mind can never know others' minds and therefore cannot be a guru. Such a person can never solve other people's problems. You have to be extremely careful before taking someone on as a guru; there are many impostors around. Westerners are sometimes too trusting. Someone comes along, "I'm a lama, I'm a yogi; I can give you knowledge," and earnest young Westerners think, "I'm sure he can teach me something. I'm going to follow him." This can really get you into trouble. I've heard of many cases of people being taken in by charlatans. Westerners tend to believe too easily. Eastern people are much more skeptical. Take your time; relax; check up.

Q: Does humility always accompany wisdom?

Lama: Yes. It's good to be as humble as possible. If you can act with both humility and wisdom all the time, your life will be wonderful. You will respect everybody.

Q: Are there exceptions to that rule? I've seen posters for one spiritual leader where it says, "I, at whose feet all people bow." Could someone who makes a statement like that be wise?

Lama: Well, it's hard to say, just like that. The point is to be as careful as you can. Our minds are funny. Sometimes we are skeptical of things that are really worthwhile and completely accepting of things that we should avoid. Try to avoid extremes and follow the middle way, checking with wisdom wherever you go. That's the most important thing.

Q: Why is there this difference between Easterners and Westerners that you mentioned?

Lama: The differences may not be all that great. Westerners might be slightly more complicated intellectually, but basically human beings are all the same; most of the time we all want to enjoy and are preoccupied by pleasures of the senses. It's at the intellectual level that our characters may differ. The differences in relation to following gurus are probably due to Asian people having had more experience in this.

Q: Is it more difficult to achieve wisdom in the West than in the East because in the West we are surrounded by too many distractions, our minds talk too much about the past, the future, and we seem to be under so much pressure? Do we have to close ourselves off completely or what?

Lama: I cannot say that gaining knowledge-wisdom in the West is more difficult than in the East. Actually, gaining wisdom, understanding your own nature, is an individual thing. You can't say it's easier in the East than in the West. Nor can you say that to develop knowledge-wisdom you have to renounce the Western material life.

You don't have to give it all up. Instead of radically abandoning every-thing, try to develop the outlook, "I need these things, but I can't say they're all I need." The problem comes when grasping and attachment dominate your mind and you put all your faith in other people and material possessions. External objects aren't the problem; the problem is the grasping mind that tells you, "I can't live without this." You can lead a life of incredible luxury but at the same time be completely detached from your possessions. The pleasure you derive from them is much greater if you enjoy them without attachment. If you can manage that, your life will be perfect. As Westerners you have the advantage of getting all these things without too much effort. In the East we really have to struggle to achieve some material comfort. As a result, there's a tendency to cling much more strongly to our posses-sions, which only results in more suffering. Either way, the problem is always attachment. Try simultaneously to be free of attachment while having it all.

I hope I have answered your questions. Thank you all so much.

Melbourne University
Melbourne, Australia
25 March 1975

A BUDDHIST APPROACH TO MENTAL ILLNESS

I was born near Lhasa, the capital of Tibet, and educated at Sera Monastic University, one of the three great monasteries in Lhasa. There they taught us how to bring an end to human problems—not so much the problems people face in their relationship to the external environment, but the internal, mental problems we all face. That was what I studied—Buddhist psychology; how to treat mental illness.

For the past ten years I have been working with Westerners, experimenting to see if Buddhist psychology also works for the Western mind. In my experience, it has been extremely effective. Recently, some of these students invited me to the West to give lectures and meditation courses, so here I am.

We lamas think that the main point is that human problems arise primarily from the mind, not from the external environment. But rather than my talking about things that you might find irrelevant, perhaps it would be better for you to ask specific questions so that I can address directly the issues that are of most interest to you.

Dr. Stan Gold: Lama, thank you very much for coming. Could I start by asking what you mean by "mental illness"?
Lama: By mental illness I mean the kind of mind that does not see reality; a mind that tends to either exaggerate or underestimate the

qualities of the person or object it perceives, which always causes problems to arise. In the West, you wouldn't consider this to be mental illness, but Western psychology's interpretation is too narrow. If someone is obviously emotionally disturbed, you consider that to be a problem, but if someone has a fundamental inability to see reality, to understand his or her own true nature, you don't. Not knowing your own basic mental attitude is a huge problem.

Human problems are more than just emotional distress or disturbed relationships. In fact, those are tiny problems. It's as if there's this huge ocean of problems below, but all we see are the small waves on the surface. We focus on those—"Oh, yes, that's a big problem"— while ignoring the actual cause, the dissatisfied nature of the human mind. It's difficult to see, but we consider people who are unaware of the nature of their dissatisfied mind to be mentally ill; their minds are not healthy.

Q: Lama Yeshe, how do you go about treating mental illness? How do you help people with mental illness?
Lama: Yes, good, wonderful. My way of treating mental illness is to try to have the person analyze the basic nature of his own problem. I try to show him the true nature of his mind so that with his own mind he can understand his own problems. If he can do that, he can solve his own problems himself. I don't believe that I can solve his problems by simply talking to him a little. That might make him feel a bit better, but it's very transient relief. The root of his problems reaches deep into his mind; as long as it's there, changing circumstances will cause more problems to emerge.

My method is to have him check his own mind in order to gradually see its true nature. I've had the experience of giving someone a little advice and having him think, "Oh, great, my problem's gone; Lama solved it with just a few words," but that's a fabrication. He's just making it up. There's no way you can understand your own mental problems without your becoming *your* own psychologist. It's impossible.

Q: How do you help people understand their problems? How do you go about it?

Lama: I try to show them the psychological aspect of their nature, how to check their own minds. Once they know this, they can check and solve their own problems. I try to teach them an approach.

Q: What, precisely, is the method that you teach for looking at the mind's true nature?

Lama: Basically it's a form of checking, or analytical, knowledge-wisdom.

Q: Is it a kind of meditation?

Lama: Yes; analytical, or checking, meditation.

Q: How do you do that? How do you teach somebody to check?

Lama: Let me give you an example. Say I have a good feeling about somebody. I have to ask myself, "Why do I feel good about this person? What makes me feel this way?" By investigating this I might find that it's just because he was nice to me once, or that there's some other similar small, illogical reason. "I love him because he did this or that." It's the same thing if I feel bad about someone; I don't like him because he did such and such. But if you look more deeply to see if those good or bad qualities really exist within the person you may see that your discrimination of friend or enemy is based on very superficial, illogical reasoning. You're basing your judgment on insignificant qualities, not on the totality of the other person's being. You see some quality you label as good or bad, perhaps something the person said or did, and then exaggerate it out of all proportion. Then you become agitated by what you perceive. Through checking you can see that there's no reason to discriminate in the way that you do; it only keeps you fettered, uptight and in suffering. This kind of checking analyzes not the other person but your own mind, in order to see how you feel and to determine what kind of discriminating mind makes you feel that way. This is a fundamentally different approach to analysis from the Western one, which focuses excessively on external factors and not enough on the part played by the mind in people's experience.

Q: So you say that the problem lies more within the person and don't agree with the point of view that it is society that makes people sick?
Lama: Yes. For example, I have met many Western people who've had problems with society. They're angry with society, with their parents, with everything. When they understand the psychology I teach, they think, "Ridiculous! I've always blamed society, but actually the *real* problem has been inside of me all along." Then they become courteous human beings, respectful of society, their parents, their teachers and all other people. You can't blame society for our problems.

Q: Why do people mix things up like that?

Lama: It's because they don't know their own true nature. The environment, ideas and philosophies can be contributory causes, but primarily, problems come from one's own mind. Of course, the way society is organized can agitate some people, but the issues are usually small. Unfortunately, people tend to exaggerate them and get upset. This is how it is with society, but anyone who thinks the world can exist without it is dreaming.

Q: Lama, what do you find in the ocean of a person's nature?
Lama: When I use that expression I'm saying that people's problems are like an ocean, but we see only the superficial waves. We don't see what lies beneath them. "Oh, I have a problem with him. If I get rid of him I'll solve my problems." It's like looking at electrical appliances without understanding that it's the underlying electricity that makes them function.

Q: What kind of problems do we find below the waves?
Lama: Dissatisfaction. The dissatisfied mind is the fundamental element of human nature. We're dissatisfied with ourselves; we're dissatisfied with the outside world. That dissatisfaction is like an ocean.

Q: Do you ask the other person questions about himself or how he feels to help him understand himself?
Lama: Sometimes we do, but usually we don't. Some people have quite specific problems; in such cases it can help to know exactly what those problems are so that we can offer precise solutions. But it's not usually necessary because basically, everybody's problems are the same.

Q: How much time do you spend talking with that person to find out about his problem and how to deal with it? As you know, in Western psychiatry, we spend a great deal of time with patients to help them discover the nature of their problems for themselves. Do you do the same thing or do you do it differently?

Lama: Our methods don't require us to spend much time with people individually. We explain the fundamental nature of problems and the possibility of transcending them; then we teach basic techniques of working with problems. They practice these techniques; after a while we check to see what their experience has been.

Q: You're saying that basically, everybody has the same problems?

Lama: Yes, right. East, West, it's basically the same thing. But in the West, people have to be clinically ill before you'll say that they're sick. That's too superficial for us. According to Lord Buddha's psychology and lamas' experience, sickness runs deeper than just the overt expression of clinical symptoms. As long as the ocean of dissatisfaction remains within you, the slightest change in the environment can be enough to bring out a problem. As far as we're concerned, even being susceptible to future problems means that your mind is not healthy. All of us here are basically the same, in that our minds are dissatisfied. As a result, a tiny change in our external circumstances can make us sick. Why? Because the basic problem is within our minds. It's much more important to eradicate the basic problem than to spend all our time trying to deal with superficial, emotional ones. This approach doesn't cease our continual experience of problems; it merely substitutes a new problem for the one we believe we've just solved.

Q: Is my basic problem the same as his basic problem?

Lama: Yes, everybody's basic problem is what we call ignorance—not understanding the nature of the dissatisfied mind. As long you have this kind of mind, you're in the same boat as everybody else. This inability to see reality is not an exclusively Western problem or an exclusively Eastern problem. It's a human problem.

Q: The basic problem is not knowing the nature of your mind?

Lama: Right, yes.

Q: And everybody's mind has the same nature?

Lama: Yes, the same nature.

Q: Each person has the same basic problem?

Lama: Yes, but there are differences. For example, a hundred years ago, people in the West had certain kinds of problems. Largely through technological development, they solved many of them, but now different problems have arisen in their stead. That's what I'm saying. New problems replace the old ones, but they're still problems, because the basic problem remains. The basic problem is like an ocean; the ones we try to solve are just the waves. It's the same in the East. In India, problems people experience in the villages are different from those experienced by people who live in the capital, New Delhi, but they're still problems. East, West, the basic problem is the same.

Q: Lama, as I understand it, you said that the basic problem is that individuals lose touch with their own nature. How do we lose touch with our own nature? Why does it happen?

Lama: One reason is that we are preoccupied with what's going on outside of ourselves. We are so interested in what's going on in the sense world that we do not take the time to examine what's going on in our minds. We never ask ourselves why the sense world is so interesting, why things appear as they do, why we respond to them as we do. I'm not saying we should ignore the outside world, but we should expend at least an equal amount of energy analyzing our relationship with it. If we can comprehend the nature of both the subject and the object, then we can really put an end to our problems. You might feel that materially your life is perfect, but you can still ask yourself, "Does this really satisfy me? Is this all there is?" You can check your mind, "Where does satisfaction really come from?" If you understand that satisfaction does not depend only on external things, you can enjoy both material possessions and peace of mind.

Q: Is the nature of each person's satisfaction different or is it the same for people in general?

Lama: Relatively speaking, each individual has his or her own way of thinking, feeling and discriminating; therefore each person's enjoyment is an individual thing. Relatively. But if you check more deeply, if you look into the profound, unchangeable, more lasting levels of feeling, happiness and joy, you will see that everybody can attain identical levels of enjoyment. In the relative, mundane world we think, "My interests and pleasures are such and such, therefore I have to have this, this and this. If I find myself in so and so circumstances, I'll be miserable." Relatively, our experiences are individual; each of us discriminates in our own way. But absolutely, we can experience an identical level of happiness.

Q: Lama, do you solve people's problems by getting them to withdraw into meditation or cut themselves off from the outside world? Is this the way you treat people?

Lama: Not necessarily. People should be totally aware of both what's going on in their own minds and how their minds are relating to the outside world, what effect the environment is having on their minds. You can't close your life off from the world; you have to face it; you have to be open to everything.

Q: Is your treatment always successful?

Lama: No. Not necessarily.

Q: What makes it unsuccessful in certain cases?

Lama: Sometimes there's a problem in communication; people misunderstand what I'm saying. Perhaps people don't have the patience to put the methods I recommend into action. It takes time to treat the dissatisfied mind. Changing the mind isn't like painting a house. You can change the color of a house in an hour. It takes a lot longer than that to transform an attitude of mind.

Q: What sort of time are you talking about? Months? Years?

Lama: It depends on the individual and the kind of problem we're talking about. If you're having a problem with your parents, maybe you can solve it in a month. But changing and overcoming the fundamentally dissatisfied mind can take many, many years. The waves are easy; the ocean is more difficult. Thank you, that was a very good question.

Q: Do you have any process by which you select the people that you might try to help?

Lama: No, we have no process of selection.

Q: People just come to you?

Lama: Yes. Anybody can come. Irrespective of color, race, class or gender, all human beings have the same potential to solve their problems. There's no problem that cannot be solved by human wisdom. If you are wise, you can solve them all.

Q: What about people who are not so wise?

Lama: Then you have to teach people how to be wise. Wisdom isn't intuitive; you have to open people's minds to it.

Q: Can you help children to solve problems in this way?

Lama: That's definitely possible. But with children you can't always intellectualize. Sometimes you have to show them things through art or by your actions. Sometimes it's not so wise to tell them to do this or do that.

Q: Lama, what sort of advice would you give parents to help their children know their inner nature?

Lama: First I'd probably say it's better not to intellectualize verbally. Acting correctly and creating a peaceful environment are much more likely to be effective. If you do, children will learn automatically. Even tiny children pick up on vibrations. I remember that when I was a small child, when my parents argued, I felt terrible; it was painful. You don't need to tell children too much but rather behave properly, peacefully and gently, and create a good environment. That's all; especially when they're too small to understand language.

Q: How important is the body in human happiness?

Lama: If you want to be happy, it's very important for your body to be healthy, because of the close link between your physical nervous system and your mind. A disturbance in your nervous system will cause a disturbance in your mind; changes in your body cause changes in your mind. There's a strong connection between the two.

Q: Do you have any advice with respect to diet or sexual behavior in keeping the body healthy?

Lama: Both can be important. Of course, we're all different, so you can't say that the same diet will suit everybody. As individuals, our bodies are habituated to particular diets, so radical dietary changes can shock our systems. Also, too much sexual activity can weaken our bodies, which in turn can weaken our minds, our power of concentration or penetrative wisdom.

Q: What is too much?

Lama: Again, that depends on the individual. It's not the same for everybody. Each person's power of body varies; check through your own experience.

Q: Why are we here? What is our reason for living?

Lama: As long as we're attached to the sense world, we're attached to our bodies, so we have to live in them.

Q: But where am I going? Do I have to go anywhere?

Lama: Yes, of course, you have no choice. You're impermanent, therefore you have to go. Your body is made up of the four ever-changing elements of earth, water, fire and air. When they're in balance, you grow properly and remain healthy. But if one of them gets out of balance with the rest, it can cause chaos in your body and end your life.

Q: And what happens then? Do we reincarnate?

Lama: Yes, we do. Your mind, or consciousness, is different from your physical body, your flesh and blood. When you die, you leave your body behind and your mind goes into a new one. Since beginningless time we've been dying and being reborn into one different body after another. That's what we understand. Lord Buddha's psychology teaches that at the relative level, the characteristic nature of the mind is quite different from that of the physical body.

Q: Do we live in order to continually improve ourselves? When you're an old man, will you be better than you are now?

Lama: You can never be sure of that. Sometimes old men are worse than children. It depends on how much wisdom you have. Some children are wiser than adults. You need wisdom to make that kind of progress during your life.

Q: If you understand yourself better in this life, do you improve in the next?

Lama: Definitely. The better you understand the nature of your mind in this life, the better your next life will be. Even in this life, if you understand your own nature well today, next month your experiences will be better.

Q: Lama, what does *nirvana* mean?

Lama: Nirvana is a Sanskrit word that means freedom, or liberation. Inner liberation. It means that your heart is no longer bound by the uncontrolled, unsubdued, dissatisfied mind, not tied by attachment. When you realize the absolute nature of your mind, you free yourself from bondage and are able to find enjoyment without dependence upon sense objects. Our minds are bound because of the conception of ego; to loosen these bonds we have to lose our ego. This might seem strange to you, that you should lose your ego. It's certainly not something we talk about in the West. On the contrary, here we are taught to build our egos; if you don't have a strong ego, you're lost, you're not human, you're weak. This seems to be society's view. However, from the point of view of Buddhist psychology, the conception of ego is our biggest problem, the king of problems; other emotions are like ministers, ego is king. When you reach beyond ego, the cabinet of other delusions disappears, the agitated, bound mind vanishes, and you attain an everlasting blissful state of mind. That's what we call nirvana, inner freedom. Your mind is no longer conditioned, tied to something else, like it is at the moment. Presently, because our mind is dependent upon other phenomena, when those other phenomena move, they take our mind with them. We have no control; our mind is led like an animal with a rope through its nose. We are not free; we have no independence. Of course, we think we're free, we think we're independent, but we're not; we're not free inside. Every time the uncontrolled mind arises, we suffer. Therefore, liberation means freedom from dependence upon other conditions and the experience of stable, everlasting bliss, instead of the up and down of our normal lives. That's nirvana. Of course, this is just a brief explanation; we could talk about it for hours, but not now. However, if you understand the nature of inner freedom, you realize that transient sense pleasures are nowhere near enough, that they're not the most important thing. You realize that as a human being you have the ability and the methods to reach a permanent state of everlasting, unconditional joy. That gives you a new perspective on life.

Q: Why do you think that the methods of Buddhist psychology offer an individual a better chance of success in achieving everlasting happiness whereas other methods may have great difficulty in doing this and sometimes never do?

Lama: I'm not saying that because Buddhist methods work we don't need any others. People are different; individual problems require individual solutions. One method won't work for everybody. In the West, you can't say that Christianity offers a solution to all human problems, therefore we don't need psychology or Hinduism or any other philosophy. That's wrong. We need a variety of methods because different people have different personalities and different emotional problems. But the real question we have to ask of any method is can it really put a complete stop to human problems for ever? Actually, Lord Buddha himself taught an amazing variety of psychological remedies to a vast range of problems. Some people think that Buddhism is a rather small subject. In fact, Lord Buddha offered billions of solutions to the countless problems people face. It's almost as if a personalized solution has been given to each individual.

Buddhism never says there's just one solution to every problem, that "This is the only way." Lord Buddha gave an incredible variety of solutions to cover every imaginable human problem. Nor is any particular problem necessarily solved all at once. Some problems have to be overcome gradually, by degrees. Buddhist methods also take this into account. That's why we need many approaches.

Q: Sometimes we see patients who are so grossly disturbed that they need large doses of various drugs or just a lot of time before you can even communicate with them. How do you approach someone with whom you can't even communicate intellectually?

Lama: First we try slowly, slowly to become friends in order to earn their trust. Then, when they improve, we start to communicate. Of course, it doesn't always work. The environment is also important—a quiet house in the country; a peaceful place, appropriate pictures, therapeutic colors, that kind of thing. It's difficult.

Q: Some Western psychologists believe that aggression is an important and necessary part of human nature, that anger is a kind of positive driving force, even though it sometimes gets people into trouble. What is your view of anger and aggression?

Lama: I encourage people not to express their anger, not to let it out. Instead, I have people try to understand why they get angry, what causes it and how it arises. When you realize these things, instead of manifesting externally, your anger digests itself. In the West, some people believe that you get rid of anger by expressing it, that you finish it by letting it out. Actually, in this case what happens is that you leave an imprint in your mind to get angry again. The effect is just the opposite of what they believe. It looks like your anger escaped but in fact you're just collecting more anger in your mind. The imprints that anger leaves on your consciousness simply reinforce your tendency to respond to situations with more anger. But not allowing it to come out doesn't mean you are suppressing it, bottling it up. That's also dangerous. You have to learn to investigate the deeper nature of anger, aggression, anxiety or whatever it is that troubles you. When you look into the deeper nature of negative energy you'll see that it's really quite insubstantial, that it's only mind. As your mental expression changes, the negative energy disappears, digested by the wisdom that understands the nature of hatred, anger, aggression and so forth.

Q: Where did the very first moment of anger come from? The anger that left imprint after imprint after imprint?
Lama: Anger comes from attachment to sense pleasure. Check up. This is wonderful psychology, but it can be difficult to understand. When someone touches something to which you are very attached, you freak out. Attachment is the source of anger.

Dr. Gold: Well, Lama, thank you very much for coming and visiting with us. It's been very, very interesting.

Lama: Thank you so much, I'm very happy to have met you all.

Prince Henry's Hospital
Melbourne, Australia
25 March 1975

EVERYTHING COMES FROM THE MIND

Buddhism can be understood on many different levels. People who actualize the Buddhist path do so gradually. Just as you pass slowly through school and university, graduating from one year to the next, so do Buddhist practitioners proceed step by step along the path to enlightenment. In Buddhism, however, we're talking about different levels of mind; here, higher and lower refer to spiritual progress.

In the West, there's a tendency to consider Buddhism as a religion in the Western sense of the term. This is a misconception. Buddhism is completely open; we can talk about anything. Buddhism has its doctrine and philosophy, but it also encourages scientific experimentation, both inner and outer. Don't think of Buddhism as some kind of narrow, closed-minded belief system. It isn't. Buddhist doctrine is not a historical fabrication derived through imagination and mental speculation, but an accurate psychological explanation of the actual nature of the mind.

When you look at the outside world you have a very strong impression of its substantiality. You probably don't realize that the strong impression is merely your own mind's interpretation of what it sees. You think that the strong, solid reality really exists outside, and perhaps, when you look within, you feel empty. This is also a misconception: the strong impression that the world appears to truly exist outside of you is actually projected by your own mind. Everything you experience—feelings, sensations, shapes and colors—comes from your mind.

Whether you get up one morning with a foggy mind and the world around you appears to be dark and foggy, or you awaken with a clear mind and your world seems beautiful and light, understand that these different impressions are coming from your own mind rather than from changes in the external environment. Instead of misinterpreting whatever you experience in life through wrong conceptions, realize that it's not outer reality, but only mind.

For example, when everybody in this auditorium looks at a single object—me, Lama Yeshe—each of you has a distinctly different experience, even though simultaneously you are all looking at the one thing. These different experiences don't come from me; they come from your own minds. Perhaps you're thinking, "Oh, how can he say that? We all see the same face, the same body, the same clothes," but that's just a superficial interpretation. Check deeper. You'll see that the way you perceive me, the way you feel, is individual, and that at that level, you're all different. These various perceptions do not come from me but from your own minds. That's the point I'm making.

Then the thought might arise, "Oh, he's just a lama; all he knows about is mind. He doesn't know about powerful scientific advances like satellites and other sophisticated technology. There's no way you can say that those things come from mind." But you check up. When I say "satellite," you have a mental image of the object that you've been told is a satellite. When the first satellite was made, its inventor said, "I've made this thing that orbits the earth; it's called a 'satellite.'" Then when everybody else saw it, they thought, "Ah, that's a satellite." But "satellite" is just a name, isn't it?

Before the inventor of the satellite actually made it, he speculated and visualized it in his mind. On the basis of this image, he acted to materialize his creation. Then he told everyone, "This is a satellite." So everyone thought, "Wow, a satellite; how beautiful, how wonderful." That shows how ridiculous we are. People give things names and we grasp at the name, believing it to be the real thing. It's the same thing no matter what colors and forms we grasp at. You check up.

If you can understand what I'm explaining here, you'll see that indeed, satellites and so forth do come from the mind, and that without mind, there is not a single manifest material existence in the entire sense world. What exists without mind? Look at all the stuff you find in supermarkets: so many names, so many foods, so many different things. First people made it all up—this name, that name, this, this, this—so then, this, that, this, this and this all appear to you. If all these thousands of supermarket items as well as jets, rockets and satellites are manifestations of mind, what then does not come from mind?

If you check into how your mind expresses itself, your various views and feelings, your imagination, you will realize that all your emotions, the way you live your life, the way you relate to others, all come from your own mind. If you don't understand how your mind works, you're going to continue having negative experiences like anger and depression. Why do I call a depressed mind negative? Because a depressed mind doesn't understand how it works. A mind without understanding is negative. A negative mind brings you down because all its reactions are polluted. A mind with understanding functions clearly. A clear mind is a positive mind.

Any emotional problem you experience arises because of the way your mind functions; your basic problem lies in the way you misidentify yourself. Do you normally hold yourself in low esteem, see yourself as a poor quality human being, while what you really want is for your life to be of the highest quality, to be perfect? You don't want to be a poor quality human being, do you? To correct your view and become a better person, you don't need to squeeze yourself or to jump from your own culture into another. All you need to do is to understand your true nature, the way you already are. That's all. It's so simple.

What I'm talking about here is not Tibetan culture, some Eastern trip. I'm talking about your trip. Actually, it doesn't matter whose trip I'm talking about; we're all basically the same. How are we different? We all have mind; we all perceive things through our senses; we are all equal in wanting to enjoy the sense world; and equally we all grasp at the sense world, knowing neither the reality of our inner world nor that of the outer one. There's no difference, whether we have long hair or short, whether we're black, white or red, no matter what clothes we wear. We're all the same. Why? Because the human mind is like an ocean and we're very similar to each other in the way we've evolved on this earth.

Superficial observation of the sense world might lead you to believe that people's problems are different, but if you check more deeply, you will see that fundamentally, they are the same. What makes people's problems appear to be unique is their different interpretation of their experiences.

This way of checking reality is not necessarily a spiritual exercise. You neither have to believe nor deny that you have a mind—all you have to do is observe how it functions and how you act, and not obsess too much about the world around you.

Lord Buddha never put much emphasis on belief. Instead, he exhorted us to investigate and try to understand the reality of our own being. He never stressed that we had to know what he was, what a buddha is. All he wanted was for us to understand our own nature. Isn't that so simple? We don't have to believe in anything. Simply by making the right effort, we understand things through our own experience, and gradually develop all realizations.

But perhaps you have a question: what about mountains, trees and oceans? How can they come from the mind? I'm going to ask you: what is the nature of a mountain? What is the nature of an ocean? Do things necessarily exist as you see them? When you look at mountains and oceans, they appear to your superficial view as mountains and oceans. But their nature is actually something else. If a hundred people look at a mountain at the same time, they all see different aspects, different colors, different features. Then whose view of the mountain is correct? If you can answer that, you can reply to your own question.

In conclusion, I'm saying that your everyday, superficial view of the sense world does not reflect its true reality. The way you interpret Melbourne, your imagination of how Melbourne exists, has nothing whatsoever to do with the reality of Melbourne—even though you might have been born in Melbourne and have spent your entire up and down life in Melbourne. Check up.

In saying all this, I'm not making a definitive statement but rather offering you a suggestion of how to look at things afresh. I'm not trying to push my own ideas onto you. All I'm doing is recommending that you set aside your usual sluggish mind, which simply takes what it sees at face value, and check with a different mind, a fresh mind.

Most of the decisions that your mind has been making from the time you were born—"This is right; this is wrong; this is not reality"—have been misconceptions. A mind possessed by misconceptions is an uncertain mind, never sure of anything. A small change in the external conditions and it freaks out; even small things make it crazy. If you could only see the whole picture, you'd see how silly this is. But we don't see totality; totality is too big for us.

The wise mind—knowledge-wisdom, or universal consciousness—is never fazed by small things. Seeing totality, it never pays attention to minutiae. Some energy coming from here clashing with some other energy from there never upsets the wise because they expect things like that to happen; it's in their nature. If you have the misconception that your life will be perfect, you will always be shocked by its up and down nature. If you expect your life to be up and down, your mind will be much more peaceful. What in the external world is perfect? Nothing. So since the energy of your mind and body are inextricably bound up with the external world, how can you expect your life to go perfectly? You can't.

Thank you so much. I hope you've understood what I've been saying and that I have not created more wrong conceptions. We have to finish now. Thank you.

Latrobe University
Melbourne, Australia
27 March 1975

MAKE YOUR MIND AN OCEAN

Look into your mind. If you fervently believe that all your enjoyment comes from material objects and dedicate your entire life to their pursuit, you're under the control of a serious misconception. This attitude is not simply an intellectual thing. When you first hear this, you might think, "Oh, I don't have that kind of mind; I don't have complete faith that external objects will bring me happiness." But check more deeply in the mirror of your mind. You will find that beyond the intellect, such an attitude is indeed there and that your everyday actions show that deep within, you really do believe this misconception. Take a moment now to check within yourself to see whether or not you really are under the influence of such an inferior mind.

A mind that has such strong faith in the material world is narrow, limited; it has no space. Its nature is sick, unhealthy, or, in Buddhist terminology, dualistic.

In many countries people are afraid of those who act out of the ordinary, such as those who use drugs. They make laws against the use of drugs and set up elaborate customs controls to catch people smuggling them into the country. Examine this more closely. Drug taking doesn't come from the drug itself but from the person's mind. It would be more sensible to be afraid of the psychological attitude—the polluted mind—that makes people take drugs or engage in other self-

51

destructive behavior, but instead, we make a lot of fuss about the drugs themselves, completely ignoring the role of the mind. This, too, is a serious misconception, much worse than the drugs a few people take.

Misconceptions are much more dangerous than just a few drugs. Drugs themselves don't spread too far, but misconceptions can spread everywhere and cause difficulty and unrest throughout an entire country. All this comes from the mind. The problem is that we don't understand the psychological nature of the mind. We pay attention to only the physical substances that people take; we're totally unaware of the stupid ideas and polluted misconceptions that are crossing borders all the time.

All mental problems come from the mind. We have to treat the mind rather than tell people, "Oh, you're unhappy because you're feeling weak. What you need is a powerful new car..." or some other kind of material possession. Telling people to go buy something to be happy is not wise advice. The person's basic problem is mental dissatisfaction, not a lack of material possessions. When it comes to the approach to mental problems and how to treat patients, there's a big difference between Lord Buddha's psychology and that which is practiced in the West.

When the patient returns and says, "Well, I bought the car you recommended but I'm still unhappy," perhaps the doctor will say, "You should have bought a more expensive one" or "You should have chosen a better color." Even if he goes away and does that, he's still going to come back unhappy. No matter how many superficial changes are made to a person's environment, his problems won't stop. Buddhist psychology recommends that, instead of constantly substituting one agitated condition for another—thereby simply changing one problem into another and then another and then another without end—give up cars completely for a while and see what happens. Sublimating one problem into another solves nothing; it's merely change. Though change may often be enough to fool people into thinking they're getting better, they're not. Basically they're still experiencing the same thing. Of course, I don't mean all this literally. I'm simply trying to illustrate how people try to solve mental problems through physical means.

Recognize the nature of your mind. As human beings, we always seek satisfaction. By knowing the nature of the mind, we can satisfy ourselves internally; perhaps even eternally. But you must realize the nature of your own mind. We see the sense world so clearly, but we're completely blind to our internal world, where the constant functioning of misconceptions keeps us under the control of unhappiness and dissatisfaction. This is what we must discover.

It is crucial, therefore, to make sure that you are not laboring under the misconception that only external objects can give you satisfaction or make your life worthwhile. As I said before, this belief is not simply intellectual—the long root of this delusion reaches deep into your mind. Many of your strongest desires are buried far below your intellect; that which lies beneath the intellect is usually much stronger than the intellect itself.

Some people might think, "My basic psychology is sound. I don't have faith in materials; I'm a student of religion." Simply having learned some religious philosophy or doctrine doesn't make you a spiritual person. Many university professors can give clear intellectual explanations of Buddhism, Hinduism and Christianity, but that alone doesn't make them spiritual people. They're more like tourist guides for the spiritually curious. If you can't put your words into experience, your learning helps neither yourselves nor others. There's a big difference between being able to explain religion intellectually and transforming that knowledge into spiritual experience.

You have to put what you've learned into your own experience and understand the results that various actions bring. A cup of tea is probably of more use than learned scholarship of a philosophy that cannot support your mind because you don't have the key—at least it quenches your thirst. Studying a philosophy that doesn't function is a waste of time and energy.

I hope that you understand what the word "spiritual" really means. It means to search for, to investigate, the true nature of the mind. There's nothing spiritual outside. My rosary isn't spiritual; my robes aren't spiritual. Spiritual means the mind, and spiritual people are those who seek its nature. Through this, they come to understand the effects of their behavior, the actions of their body, speech and mind. If you don't understand the karmic results of what you think and do, there's no way for you to become a spiritual person. Just knowing some religious philosophy isn't enough to make you spiritual.

To enter the spiritual path, you must begin to understand your own mental attitude and how your mind perceives things. If you're all caught up in attachment to tiny atoms, your limited, craving mind will make it impossible for you to enjoy life's pleasures. External energy is so incredibly limited that if you allow yourself to be bound by it, your mind itself will become just as limited. When your mind is narrow, small things agitate you very easily. Make your mind an ocean.

We hear religious people talk a lot about morality. What is morality? Morality is the wisdom that understands the nature of the mind. The mind that understands its own nature automatically becomes moral, or positive; and the actions motivated by such a mind also become positive. That's what we call morality. The basic nature of the narrow mind is ignorance; therefore the narrow mind is negative.

If you know the psychological nature of your own mind, depression is spontaneously dispelled; instead of being enemies and strangers, all living beings become your friends. The narrow mind rejects; wisdom accepts. Check your own mind to see whether or not this is true. Even if you were to get every possible sense pleasure that the universe could offer, you would still not be satisfied. That shows that satisfaction comes from within, not from anything external.

Sometimes we marvel at the modern world: "What fantastic advances scientific technology has made; how wonderful! We never had these things before." But step back and take another look. Many of the things we thought fantastic not so long ago are now rising up against us. Things we developed to help our lives are now hurting us. Don't just look at your immediate surroundings, but check as widely as possible; you'll see the truth of what I'm saying. When we first create material things we think, "Oh, this is useful." But gradually this external energy turns inward and destroys itself. Such is the nature of the four elements: earth, water, fire and air. This is what Buddhist science teaches us.

Your body is no exception to this rule. As long as your elements are cooperating with each other, your body grows beautifully. But after a while the elements turn against themselves and finish up destroying your life. Why does this happen? Because of the limited nature of material phenomena: when their power is exhausted, they collapse, like the old and crumbling buildings we see around us.

When our bodies become sick and decrepit it's a sign that our internal energies are in conflict, out of balance. This is the nature of the material world; it has nothing to do with faith. As long as we keep being born into the meat, blood and bone of the human body, we're going to experience bad conditions, whether we believe it or not. This is the natural evolution of the worldly body.

The human mind, however, is completely different. The human mind has the potential for infinite development. If you can discover, even in a small way, that true satisfaction comes from your mind, you will realize that you can extend this experience without limit and that it is possible to discover everlasting satisfaction.

It's actually very simple. You can check for yourself right now. Where do you experience the feeling of satisfaction? In your nose? Your eye? Your head? Your lung? Your heart? Your stomach? Where is that feeling of satisfaction? In your leg? Your hand? Your brain? No! It's in your mind. If you say it's in your brain, why can't you say it's in your nose or your leg? Why do you differentiate? If your leg hurts, you feel it down there, not inside your head. Anyway, whatever pain, pleasure or other feeling you experience, it's all an expression of mind.

When you say, "I had a good day today," it shows that you're holding in your mind the memory of a bad day. Without the mind creating labels, there's neither good experience nor bad. When you say that tonight's dinner was good, it means that you're holding the experience of a bad dinner in mind. Without the experience of a bad dinner it's impossible for you to call tonight's good.

Similarly, "I'm a good husband," "I'm a bad wife," are also merely expressions of mind. Someone who says, "I am bad" is not necessarily bad; someone who says, "I am good" is not necessarily good. Perhaps the man who says, "I'm such a good husband" does so because his mind is full of the disturbing negative mind of pride. His narrow mind, stuck in the deluded, concrete belief that he's good, actually causes much difficulty for his wife. How, then, is he a good husband? Even if he does provide food and clothing for his wife, how can he be a good husband, when day after day she has to live with his arrogance?

If you can understand the psychological aspects of human problems, you can really generate true loving-kindness towards others. Just talking about loving-kindness doesn't help you develop it. Some people may have read about loving-kindness hundreds of times but their minds are the very opposite. It's not just philosophy, not just words; it's knowing how the mind functions. Only then can you develop loving-kindness; only then can you become a spiritual person. Otherwise, though you might be convinced you're a spiritual person, it's just intellectual, like the arrogant man who believes he's a good husband. It's a fiction; your mind just makes it up.

It is so worthwhile that you devote your precious human life to controlling your mad elephant mind and giving direction to your powerful mental energy. If you don't harness your mental energy, confusion will continue to rage through your mind and your life will be completely wasted. Be as wise with your own mind as you possibly can. That makes your life worthwhile.

I don't have much else to tell you, but if you have any questions, please ask.

Q: I understand what you said about knowing the nature of your own mind bringing you happiness, but you used the term "everlasting," which implies that if you understand your mind completely, you can transcend death of the physical body. Is this correct?

Lama: Yes, that's right. But that's not all. If you know how, when negative physical energy arises, you can convert it into wisdom. In this way your negative energy digests itself and doesn't end up blocking your psychic nervous system. That's possible.

Q: Is the mind body, or is the body mind?

Lama: What do you mean?

Q: Because I perceive the body.

Lama: Because you perceive it? Do you perceive this rosary [holding it up]?

Q: Yes.

Lama: Does that make it mind? Because you perceive it?

Q: That's what I'm asking you.

Lama: Well, that's a good question. Your body and mind are very strongly connected; when something affects your body it also affects your mind. But that doesn't mean that the relative nature of your physical body, its meat and bone, is mind. You can't say that.

Q: What are the aims of Buddhism: enlightenment, brotherhood, universal love, super consciousness, realization of the truth, the attainment of nirvana?

Lama: All of the above: super consciousness, the fully awakened state of mind, universal love, and an absence of partiality or bias based on the realization that all living beings throughout the universe are equal in wanting to be happy and to avoid feeling unhappy. At the moment, our dualistic, wrong-conception minds discriminate: "This is my close friend, I want to keep her for myself and not share her with others." One of Buddhism's aims is to attain the opposite of this, universal love. Of course, the ultimate goal is enlightenment. In short, the aim of Lord Buddha's teachings on the nature of the mind is for us to gain all those realizations you mentioned.

Q: But which is considered to be the highest or most important aim?
Lama: The highest aims are enlightenment and the development of universal love. The narrow mind finds it difficult to experience such realizations.

Q: In Tibetan paintings, how do colors correspond with states of meditation or different psychological states?
Lama: Different kinds of mind perceive different colors. We say that when we are angry we see red. That's a good example. Other states of mind visualize their own respective colors. In some cases, where people are emotionally disturbed and unable to function in their daily lives, surrounding them with certain colors can help settle them down. If you think about this you will discover that color really comes from the mind. When you get angry and see red, is that color internal or external? Think about it.

Q: What are the practical, daily life implications of your saying that in order to have the idea that something is good you must also have in your mind the idea of bad?
Lama: I was saying that when you interpret things as good or bad it's

your own mind's interpretation. What's bad for you is not necessarily bad for me.

Q: But my bad is still my bad.
Lama: Your bad is bad for you because your mind calls it bad.

Q: Can I go beyond that?
Lama: Yes, you can go beyond that. You have to ask and answer the question, "Why do I call this bad?" You have to question both the object and the subject, both the external and the internal situations. In that way you can realize that the reality is somewhere in between, that in the space between the two there's a unified mind. That's wisdom.

Q: How old were you when you entered the monastery?
Lama: I was six.

Q: What is nirvana?
Lama: When you transcend the wrong-conception, agitated mind and attain fully integrated, everlastingly satisfied wisdom, you have reached nirvana.

Q: Every religion says that it is the one way to enlightenment. Does Buddhism recognize all religions as coming from the same source?
Lama: There are two ways of answering that question, the absolute and the relative. Religions that emphasize the attainment of enlightenment are probably talking about the same thing, but where they differ is in their approach, in their methods. I think this is helpful. But it's also true that some religions may be based on misconceptions.

Nevertheless, I don't repudiate them. For example, a couple of thousand years ago there were some ancient Hindu traditions that believed the sun and moon to be gods; some of them still exist. From my point of view, those conceptions are wrong, but I still say that they're good. Why? Because even though philosophically they're incorrect, they still teach the basic morality of being a good human being and not harming others. That gives their followers the possibility of reaching the point where they discover for themselves, "Oh, I used to believe that the sun was a god but now I see I was wrong." Therefore, there's good in every religion and we should not judge, "This is totally right; that is totally wrong."

Q: As far as you know, what is life like for people in Tibet these days? Are they free to pursue their Buddhist religion as before?

Lama: They are not free and are completely prohibited from any religious practice. The Chinese authorities are totally against anything to do with religion. Monasteries have been destroyed and sacred scriptures burned.

Q: But even though their books have been burned, do the older people still keep the Dharma in their hearts and minds, or have they forgotten everything?

Lama: It's impossible to forget, to separate their minds from such powerful wisdom. So the Dharma remains in their hearts.

Q: All religions, for example, Hinduism, teach their adherents to avoid evil actions and to practice good ones and that good karmic results will ensue. How, according to Buddhism, does this accumulation of positive karma help one attain enlightenment?

Lama: Mental development does not happen through radical change. Defilements are eliminated, or purified, slowly, slowly. There's a gradual evolution. It takes time. Some people, for instance, cannot accept what Buddhism teaches about universal love, that you should want others to have the happiness that you want for yourself. They feel, "It's impossible for me to love all others as I love myself." It takes time for them to realize universal love or enlightenment because their minds are preoccupied by misconceptions and there's no space for wisdom. But slowly, slowly, through practicing their religion, people can be led to perfect wisdom. That's why I say that a variety of religions is necessary for the human race. Physical change is easy, but mental development takes time. For example, a doctor might tell a sick person, "Your temperature is very high, so please avoid meat and eat only dry biscuits for a few days." Then, as the person starts to recover, the doctor slowly reintroduces heavy food into his diet. In that way the doctor gradually leads the person back to perfect health.

Q: When Tibetan monks and nuns die, do their bodies disappear, do they take their bodies with them?

Lama: Yes, they carry them to their next lives in their *jola* [monk's shoulder bag]...I'm joking! No, that's impossible. Still, there are certain practitioners whose bodies are digested into wisdom and actually disappear. That's possible. But they don't take their bodies with them physically.

Q: Since our minds can deceive us, and without a teacher we can't discover the truth, are Buddhist monasteries designed so that each monk pulls his colleagues up to the next step of knowledge, in a sort of chain? Is that what you're doing now, and do you teach in order to learn?

Lama: Yes, monasteries are something like that, and it's also true that I learn as I teach. But why we need teachers is because book knowledge is just dry information and if left as such can be as relevant as the wind whistling through the trees. We need a key to put it into experience, to unify that knowledge with our minds. Then knowledge becomes wisdom and the perfect solution to problems. For example, the Bible is an excellent book that contains all kinds of great methods, but if you don't have the key, the knowledge that's in the Bible doesn't enter your heart. Just because a book is excellent doesn't necessarily mean that by reading it you'll gain the knowledge it contains. The only way that can happen is for your mind to first develop wisdom.

Q: You said that getting enlightened is a gradual process, but surely you can't be both enlightened and unenlightened at the same time. Wouldn't that mean, therefore, that enlightenment is sudden?

Lama: Of course, you're right. You can't be enlightened and ignorant together. Approaching enlightenment is a gradual process, but once you attain it, there's no going back; when you reach the fully awakened state of mind, the moment you experience that, you remain enlightened forever. It's not like some hallucinatory drug experience—when you're high you're having a good time, and when the effect of the drug wears off you're back down to your usual depressed self.

Q: And we can experience that in this life, permanent enlightenment, while we're still alive, before we die?

Lama: Yes, that's possible. In this life…if you have enough wisdom.

Q: Oh…if you have enough wisdom?

Lama: Yes…that's the catch: if you have enough wisdom.

Q: Why do we need a teacher?

Lama: Why do you need an English teacher? For communication. It's the same thing with enlightenment. Enlightenment is also communication. Even for mundane activities like shopping we need to learn the language so that we can communicate with the shopkeepers. If we need teachers for that, of course we need someone to guide us along a path that deals with so many unknowns like past and future lives and deep levels of consciousness. These are entirely new experiences; you don't know where you're going or what's happening. You need someone to make sure you're on the right track and not hallucinating.

Q: Who taught the first teacher?

Lama: Wisdom. The first teacher was wisdom.

Q: Well, if the first teacher didn't have a human teacher, why do any of us need one?

Lama: Because there's no beginning, and there's no end. Wisdom is universal wisdom, wisdom is universal consciousness.

Q: Does generating universal love bring you to enlightenment or do you first have to reach enlightenment and then generate universal love?

Lama: First you generate universal love. Then your mind attains the realization of equilibrium, where you emphasize neither this nor that. Your mind attains a state of balance. In Buddhist terminology, you reach beyond the dualistic mind.

Q: Is it true that the mind can only take you so far on the spiritual path and that at some point, in order to go further, you have to give up your mind?

Lama: How can you give up your mind? I'm joking. No, it's impossible for you to abandon your mind. While you're a human, living what we call an ordinary life, you have mind; when you reach enlightenment, you still have mind. Your mind is always with you. You can't get rid of it simply by saying, "I don't want to have a mind." Karmically, your mind and body are stuck together. It's impossible to relinquish your mind intellectually. If your mind were a material phenomenon, perhaps you could, but it's not.

Q: Do lamas ever become physically ill, and if so, what method do you use to overcome the illness? Do you use healing power?

Lama: Yes, sometimes we use healing power; sometimes we use the power of mantra; sometimes we meditate. At certain other times we do *puja*. Do you know what that is? Some people think it's just ritual chanting and bell ringing, but it's much more than that. Puja is a Sanskrit word whose literal meaning is "offering"; but its interpretive meaning is wisdom, an awakened state of mind. So, if your wisdom is ringing, "ting, ting, ting," that's good, but if your wisdom isn't ringing and the only ting, ting, ting you hear is the external one, then that's no puja.

Q: What you're saying is not that far removed from Western materialist philosophy. Our problems are not so much with objects as with our attitude towards them.

Lama: When you say attitude, are you referring to the mental tendency to grasp or not to grasp at material objects?

Q: Well, external objects do exist, but they exist outside of ourselves, and our consciousness perceives them on the same plane. I believe that when we die, the objects remain, but not for us, not for the individual.
Lama: I agree with you. When we die, the external objects are still there, but our interpretation of them, our projection, disappears. Yes, that's right.

Q: So how is that so radically opposed to materialistic philosophy? Why do you say that the external world is illusory when after our consciousness departs, the material world remains?
Lama: I say that the material world is illusory because the objects you perceive exist only in the view of your own mind. Look at this table: the problem is that you think that when you disappear, your view of this table still exists, that this table continues to exist just the way you saw it. That's not true. Your view of the table disappears, but another view of the table continues to exist.

Q: How can we recognize the right teacher?
Lama: You can recognize your teacher through using your own wisdom and not just following someone blindly. Investigate potential teachers as much as you possibly can. "Is this the right teacher for me or not?" Check deeply before you follow any teacher's advice. In Tibetan we have an admonition not to take a teacher like a dog seizes a piece of meat. If you give a hungry dog a piece of meat he'll just gobble it up without hesitation. It is crucial that you examine possible spiritual leaders, teachers, gurus or whatever you call them very, very

carefully before accepting their guidance. Remember what I said before about misconceptions and polluted doctrines being more dangerous than drugs? If you follow the misconceptions of a false spiritual guide it can have a disastrous effect on you and cause you to waste not only this life but many others as well. Instead of helping you, it can bring you great harm. Please, be very wise in choosing your spiritual teacher.

Q: Since you are a Buddhist monk from Tibet, I'm wondering if you've heard of Lobsang Rampa, who has written many detailed books about Tibet despite having never been there himself? He's dead now, but he said that the spirit of a Tibetan lama entered him and that's how he could write what he did. Is that possible, and if not, how could he have written those books?

Lama: I don't think that this kind of possession is possible. Also, you should check what he wrote more carefully; there are many mistakes in his books. For example, when he talks about lamas opening the wisdom eye he says it's done surgically. That's not right. The wisdom eye is a metaphor for spiritual insight and it's opened by lamas who have the key of wisdom. Also, those who have realizations don't talk about them, and those who talk about their realizations don't have them.

Q: Lama, what do you mean by dualistic mind, and what do you mean by "checking up"?

Lama: From the time you were born up to the present, two things have always complicated your mind; there are always two things, never just one. That's what we mean by the dualistic mind. Whenever you see one thing, your mind automatically, instinctively, compares it to something else: "What about that?" Those two things upset your equilibrium. That's the dualistic mind at work. Now, your other question. When I say, "check up," I mean that you should investigate your own mind to see if it's healthy or not. Every morning, check your mental state to make sure that during the day you don't freak out. That's all I mean by "check up."

Q: If everything is karmically determined, how do we know if our motivation is correct, or do we have a chance of unconditioned choice?

Lama: Pure motivation is not determined by karma. Pure motivation comes from understanding-knowledge-wisdom. If there's no understanding in your mind it's difficult for your motivation to be pure. For example, if I don't understand my own selfish nature, I can't help others. As long as I don't recognize my selfish behavior, I always blame others for my problems. When I know my own mind, my motivation becomes pure and I can sincerely dedicate the actions of my body, speech and mind to the welfare of others.

Thank you, that was a wonderful question, and I think that pure motivation is a good place to stop. Thank you so much. If we have pure motivation, we sleep well, dream well and enjoy well, so thank you very much.

Assembly Hall
Melbourne, Australia
27 March 1975

THE LAMA YESHE WISDOM ARCHIVE

The LAMA YESHE WISDOM ARCHIVE (LYWA) is the collected works of Lama Thubten Yeshe and Lama Thubten Zopa Rinpoche. The ARCHIVE was founded in 1996 by Lama Zopa Rinpoche, its spiritual director, to make available in various ways the teachings it contains. Distribution of free booklets of edited teachings is one of the ways.

Lama Yeshe and Lama Zopa Rinpoche began teaching at Kopan Monastery, Nepal, in 1970. Since then, their teachings have been recorded and transcribed. At present the LYWA contains about 6,000 cassette tapes and approximately 40,000 pages of transcribed teachings on computer disk. Many tapes by Lama Zopa Rinpoche remain to be transcribed. As Rinpoche continues to teach, the number of tapes in the ARCHIVE increases accordingly. Most of the transcripts have been neither checked nor edited.

Here at the LYWA we are making every effort to organize the transcription of that which has not yet been transcribed, to edit that which has not yet been edited, and generally to do the many other tasks detailed below. In all this, we need your help. Please contact us for more information.

THE LAMA YESHE WISDOM ARCHIVE
PO Box 356
Weston, MA 02493, USA
Telephone (781) 899-9587
email nribush@cs.com
www.LamaYeshe.com

THE ARCHIVE TRUST

The work of the LAMA YESHE WISDOM ARCHIVE falls into two categories: archiving and dissemination.

ARCHIVING requires managing the audiotapes of teachings by Lama Yeshe and Lama Zopa Rinpoche that have already been collected, collecting tapes of teachings given but not yet sent to the ARCHIVE, and collecting tapes of Lama Zopa's on-going teachings, talks, advice and so forth as he travels the world for the benefit of all. Tapes are then catalogued and stored safely while being kept accessible for further work.

We organize the transcription of tapes, add the transcripts to the already existent database of teachings, manage this database, have transcripts checked, and make transcripts available to editors or others doing research on or practicing these teachings.

Other archiving activities include working with videotapes and photographs of the Lamas and investigating the latest means of preserving ARCHIVE materials.

DISSEMINATION involves making the Lamas' teachings available directly or indirectly through various avenues such as booklets for free distribution, regular books for the trade, lightly edited transcripts, floppy disks, audio- and videotapes, and articles in *Mandala* and other magazines, and on the LYWA Web site, www.LamaYeshe.com. Irrespective of the method we choose, the teachings require a significant amount of work to prepare them for distribution.

This is just a summary of what we do. The ARCHIVE was established with virtually no seed funding and has developed solely through the kindness of many people, some of whom we have mentioned at the front of this booklet.

Our further development similarly depends upon the generosity of those who see the benefit and necessity of this work, and we would be extremely grateful for your help.

THE ARCHIVE TRUST has been established to fund the above activities and we hereby appeal to you for your kind support. If you would like to make a contribution to help us with any of the above tasks or to sponsor booklets for free distribution, please contact us at the address above.

The LAMA YESHE WISDOM ARCHIVE is a 501(c)(3) tax-deductible, non-profit corporation (ID number 04-3374479) dedicated to the welfare of all sentient beings and totally dependent upon your donations for its continued existence.

Thank you so much for your support. You may contribute by mailing us a check, bank draft or money order to our Weston address, by mailing us or phoning in your credit card number, or by transferring funds directly to our bank—details below. Thank you so much.

Bank information

Name of bank: Fleet
ABA routing number 011000390
Account: LYWA 546-81495
SWIFT address: FNBB US 33

THE FOUNDATION FOR THE PRESERVATION OF THE MAHAYANA TRADITION

The Foundation for the Preservation of the Mahayana Tradition (FPMT) is an international organization of Buddhist meditation, study and retreat centers, both urban and rural, monasteries, publishing houses, healing centers and other related activities founded in 1975 by Lama Thubten Yeshe and Lama Thubten Zopa Rinpoche. At present, there are more than 120 FPMT activities in twenty-five countries worldwide.

The FPMT has been established to facilitate the study and practice of Mahayana Buddhism in general, and the Tibetan Gelug tradition, founded in the fifteenth century by the great scholar, yogi and saint, Lama Je Tsong Khapa, in particular, for the benefit of all sentient beings.

Every two months, the Foundation publishes a magazine, *Mandala*, from its international office in the United States of America. For a sample issue of the magazine or for more information about the organization, please contact:

FPMT
PO Box 800
Soquel, CA 95073, USA
Telephone (831) 476-8435; fax (831) 476-4823
email fpmt@compuserve.com
or check out our Web site at www.fpmt.org

Our Web site also offers teachings by His Holiness the Dalai Lama, Lama Yeshe, Lama Zopa Rinpoche and many other highly respected teachers in the tradition; details of the FPMT's educational programs; a complete listing of FPMT centers all over the world and in your area; back issues of *Mandala*; and links to FPMT centers on the web, where you will find details of their programs, and to other interesting Buddhist and Tibetan home pages.

Lama Zopa Rinpoche
Teachings from the Vajrasattva Retreat
Edited by Ailsa Cameron and Nicholas Ribush

This book is an edited transcript of Rinpoche's teachings during the Vajrasattva retreat at Land of Medicine Buddha, California, February through April, 1999. It contains explanations of the various practices done during the retreat, such as Vajrasattva purification, prostrations to the Thirty-five Buddhas, Lama Chöpa, making light offerings, liberating animals and much, much more. There are also many weekend public lectures covering general topics such as compassion and emptiness. The appendices detail several of the practices taught, for example, the short Vajrasattva sadhana, light offerings, liberating animals and making charity of water to Dzambhala and the pretas.

It is essential reading for all Lama Zopa Rinpoche's students, especially retreat leaders and FPMT center spiritual program coordinators, and serious Dharma students everywhere.

704 pp., detailed table of contents, 7 appendices
6" x 9" paperback
ISBN 1-891868-04-7
US$20 & shipping and handling

Available from the LYWA, Wisdom Publications (Boston), Wisdom Books (London), Mandala Books (Melbourne), Snow Lion Publications (USA) and FPMT centers everywhere. Discount for bookstores. Free for members of the International Mahayana Institute.

OTHER TEACHINGS OF
LAMA YESHE AND LAMA ZOPA RINPOCHE
CURRENTLY AVAILABLE

BOOKS PUBLISHED BY WISDOM PUBLICATIONS

Wisdom Energy, by Lama Yeshe and Lama Zopa Rinpoche
Introduction to Tantra, by Lama Yeshe
Transforming Problems, by Lama Zopa Rinpoche
The Door to Satisfaction, by Lama Zopa Rinpoche
The Tantric Path of Purification, by Lama Yeshe
The Bliss of Inner Fire, by Lama Yeshe

A number of transcripts by Lama Yeshe and Lama Zopa are also available. For more information about these transcripts or the books mentioned above, see the Wisdom Web site (www.wisdompubs.org) or contact Wisdom directly at 199 Elm Street, Somerville, MA 02144, USA, or Wisdom distributors such as Snow Lion Publications (USA), Wisdom Books (England), or Mandala Books (Australia).

VIDEOS OF LAMA YESHE
Available in both PAL and NTSC formats.

Introduction to Tantra: 2 tapes, US$40
The Three Principal Aspects of the Path: 2 tapes, US$40
Offering Tsok to Heruka Vajrasattva: 3 tapes, US$50

Shipping and handling extra. Available from LYWA, Mandala Books, Wisdom Books, or Meridian Trust (London). Contact LYWA for more details or see our Web site, www.LamaYeshe.com

What to do with Dharma teachings

The Buddhadharma is the true source of happiness for all sentient beings. Books like this show you how to put the teachings into practice and integrate them into your life, whereby you get the happiness you seek. Therefore, anything containing Dharma teachings or the names of your teachers is more precious than other material objects and should be treated with respect. To avoid creating the karma of not meeting the Dharma again in future lives, please do not put books (or other holy objects) on the floor or underneath other stuff, step over or sit upon them, or use them for mundane purposes such as propping up wobbly tables. They should be kept in a clean, high place, separate from worldly writings, and wrapped in cloth when being carried around. These are but a few considerations.

Should you need to get rid of Dharma materials, they should not be thrown in the rubbish but burned in a special way. Briefly: do not incinerate such materials with other trash, but alone, and as they burn, recite the mantra OM AH HUM. As the smoke rises, visualize that it pervades all of space, carrying the essence of the Dharma to all sentient beings in the six samsaric realms, purifying their minds, alleviating their suffering, and bringing them all happiness, up to and including enlightenment. Some people might find this practice a bit unusual, but it is given according to tradition. Thank you very much.

Dedication

Through the merit created by preparing, reading, thinking about and sharing this book with others, may all teachers of the Dharma live long and healthy lives, may the Dharma spread throughout the infinite reaches of space, and may all sentient beings quickly attain enlightenment.

In whichever realm, country, area or place this book may be, may there be no war, drought, famine, disease, injury, disharmony or unhappiness, may there be only great prosperity, may every thing needed be easily obtained, and may all be guided by only perfectly qualified Dharma teachers, enjoy the happiness of Dharma, have only love and compassion for all beings, and only benefit and never harm each other.

LAMA THUBTEN YESHE was born in Tibet in 1935. At the age of six, he entered the great Sera Monastic University, Lhasa, where he studied until 1959, when the Chinese invasion of Tibet forced him into exile in India. Lama Yeshe continued to study and meditate in India until 1967, when, with his chief disciple, Lama Thubten Zopa Rinpoche, he went to Nepal. Two years later he established Kopan Monastery, near Kathmandu, in order to teach Buddhism to Westerners. In 1974, the Lamas began making annual teaching tours to the West, and as a result of these travels a worldwide network of Buddhist teaching and meditation centers—the Foundation for the Preservation of the Mahayana Tradition—began to develop. In 1984, after an intense decade of imparting a wide variety of incredible teachings and establishing one FPMT activity after another, at the age of forty-nine, Lama Yeshe passed away. He was reborn as Ösel Hita Torres in Spain in 1985, recognized as the incarnation of Lama Yeshe by His Holiness the Dalai Lama in 1986, and, as the monk Lama Tenzin Osel Rinpoche, began studying for his geshe degree in 1992 at the reconstituted Sera Monastery in South India. Lama's remarkable story is told in Vicki Mackenzie's book, *Reincarnation: The Boy Lama* (Wisdom Publications, 1996).

Some of Lama Yeshe's teachings have also been published by Wisdom. Books include *Wisdom Energy; Introduction to Tantra; The Tantric Path of Purification;* and (recently) *The Bliss of Inner Fire.* Transcripts in print are *Light of Dharma; Life, Death and After Death;* and *Transference of Consciousness at the Time of Death.* Available through FPMT centers or at www.wisdompubs.org.

Lama Yeshe on videotape: *Introduction to Tantra, The Three Principal Aspects of the Path,* and *Offering Tsok to Heruka Vajrasattva.* Available from the LAMA YESHE WISDOM ARCHIVE.

DR. NICHOLAS RIBUSH, MB, BS, is a graduate of Melbourne University Medical School (1964) who first encountered Buddhism at Kopan Monastery in 1972. Since then he has been a student of Lamas Yeshe and Zopa Rinpoche and a full time worker for the FPMT. He was a monk from 1974 to 1986. He established FPMT archiving and publishing activities at Kopan in 1973, and with Lama Yeshe founded Wisdom Publications in 1975. Between 1981 and 1996 he served variously as Wisdom's director, editorial director and director of development. Over the years he has edited and published many teachings by Lama Yeshe and Lama Zopa Rinpoche, and established and/or directed several other FPMT activities, including the International Mahayana Institute, Tushita Mahayana Meditation Centre, the Enlightened Experience Celebration, Mahayana Publications, Kurukulla Center for Tibetan Buddhist Studies and now the Lama Yeshe Wisdom Archive. He has been a member of the FPMT board of directors since its inception in 1983.